A Game of Polarities

Keaghan O'Connor

BookLeaf Publishing

India | USA | UK

Presentation by *BookLeaf Publishing*

Web: www.bookleafpub.com

E-mail: info@bookleafpub.com

ISBN: 9789358314939

First edition 2023

To my mother, who is my number one supported and the only reason I have not given up. Her strength inspires me every waking second. Our darkest moments in life we have been struck by cannot even compare to the happiness and blessings we have received today, which is all thanks to you.

To my 10 year old self, my 16 year old self, to myself now, and especially dedicated to who I will become 10 years down the road.

ACKNOWLEDGEMENT

I am grateful for every field I have walked upon and every hand I have shook. Every experience I have seen and every conversation I have been apart of has changed me, even if it was a slight change or a profound one, I am shaped and inspired by every living thing and every feeling I have come across.

PREFACE

This is probably the most vulnerable thing I have ever done, which is terrifying. I have always wanted to show my mind to the world to find solace, but have been afraid because of the twisted, complex, and chaotic thoughts within my soul.

The world in my head is the world I want to refurbish and preserve,
So an essence of Keaghan is woven into every word.

I wanted to create a voice for myself, so if anyone can feel seen by my words or can envision the prison I have put my mind through, then I have done a job well done.

It is not meant to be understood, hopefully someone can appreciate the chaos like I do.

2/21/17

I feel numb and completely blank.
I cannot comprehend anything, when I cannot
understand is when I cannot control, which is
terrifying.

I do not understand why I had to be born this
way, it cannot be like this forever right?
Keaghan?

I pray to my future self similarly to how I pray
to God.

Not to be sacrilegious, but I am just pleading to
everything I am hopefully looking up to for
salvation.

9/30/21

Dear 18 year old Keaghan,

Where are you? You are lost and scared and trying to find purpose right now.
I am so proud of you for not giving up.
We are 19 now, and I know you wrote to me and begged me to have it all together and find all the answers.

All I have to offer you right now is a hug and to hold onto the notion that everything means something.

We have grown so much, experienced so much, and learned so many lessons that we do not even think the same anymore.

New friendships, opportunities, and pathways of life have been revealed to us and all I can we can do is trust it. We have run for so long looking over our shoulder, I had to stop the chase.

We have created so many things, and although we are still searching desperately for answers,

we are learning that the universe will answer
each and every question in due time.

No version of ourselves can rush happiness or
try and find it, we have to be happiness itself.
We need to search within ourselves for it first,
since the search of happiness in the world can be
disappointing.

I love you so much.

2/27/23

I wish I could encapsulate my mind easier on
paper,
just to show the world!
Show the world this fucked up masterpiece.

So many more creative people than me-
but I need to find the beauty in that.

Creativity does not need to be planned or
structured all the time.
It appears after inspiration.
Creativity is the orgasam excuted from
inspiration.
Or is it the other way around?

I find it impossible to be genuinely vulnerable,
but I wish someone would want to try and dive
deeper to understand me.
I do not think I would let them, but I still desire
it.

Is that selfish of me? Or human nature?

3/9/23

Emotions aren't real, people are imitations to be
simple.
I wish I was simple.

I am searching and searching-
for what?
What is it?

The silence of sleep is the only safety for me.
I always seek shelter in instability.

I want to feel seen without fear of perception.

I genuinely think I am losing my mind!

Is it rediscovery or is it delusion?

I wonder if contentment is even a goal-
or is it simply a human feeling?

3/10/23

To understand spirit comes with appreciating humanly things and experiences.

Time is blurry and I cannot escape the fear of running out of it.

I want to manifest and materialize the love I yearn for- I am tired of feeling unlovable.

Release me from the shackles of my mind and give me strength.

3/12/23

I want growth and it is painful.
I am hurting really bad.
It is so intense it hurts my chest and flattens my
thoughts.

I cannot connect with myself as much and that is
terrifying.

I do know this will all play out in the way it is
meant to, but my heart aches for the feeling of
the future.

I am trying to stay afloat but my thoughts are
recurring and changing the tide drastically.

I realize self accountability is necessary, but I
am helpless in helping myself right now.

I want to stop feeling like I am too much, I know
how much I exhaust myself mentally, and I do
not want to give that burden to anyone.
It is heavy and too much.

Clarity is a bitch-
and so is the government.

3/12/23

Keaghan,

Force me to feel love.
Force me to let my guard down.
Force me to not be afraid.
Force me to try.

I am trying each day, but my mind is slipping.

Do people see it? Do I hide it that well?
Or do people rationalize my sickness because I
am pretty?

questions, questions, questions.

ANSWERS PLEASE!

3/13/23

I want to create the foundation of life that my
soul adores and craves for living.
I know everyone is entitled to the feeling of
individuality, but I think the vast amount of
introspection I possess, something is different in
me.

I feel as though Spirit is trying to get through to
my soul, I just don't know yet.
They are pushing me towards something, I just
know it.

One day the skeletons in my closet will be put
away neatly in the attic.

I wish I could let my persona fall to the ground
and the rawest version of myself to be valued.

3/14/23

I have so much to say but nothing to write

Time freaks me the fuck out.

My heart hurts slowly over centuries it seems,
but in the same circulation that my mind hurts as
fast as a bullet train.

I love the states of Nirvana I get to experience
when I am hollow and swallowed by my own
self.
That deep silence where the world is painfully
slow, I sickly find comfort in that, a painfully
heavy blanket.

3/14/23

I think the disappointment I feel towards myself
is the heaviest dread of all.

I am worried of my inability to remember.
Am I not meant for reflection?
Maybe I am subconsciously protecting myself
from doing so.

I need to get this out-
I hope the solution or salvation crosses my mind
soon.
Im praying it comes off the messy railroad of my
thoughts prominently enough that I catch it.
The train does not stop for anything, or anyone.

9/15/23

I love self reflection so much that I hate it.
I have always ran deep into my mind for
salvation, ironically I want to run away from my
head.
Is my heart too heavy to be carried to safety?
Or is my heart stuck in the crossfire of the war in
my head?

So dramatic!
The wide range of experiences and emotion!

It's almost comforting how much hurt is in the
world,
because pain is universal
We have all been kissed by this.
We are all wrapped into it.

Crazy how alone one can feel-
Crazy how alone we really are.

As always, perspective will inevitably say
otherwise.

3/20/23

The irony of my self sabotage!

My desire for pleasure and my obsessive
tendency somewhat disgusts me.

Intimacy is intensely woven into my soul that it
scares me.
I crave connection so bad but am terrified of it.

I have to accept that the fantasy of someone
coming to save me is not going to happen, I have
to be my own knight
Definitely not in shining armour but a knight at
the very least.

I am a duality at the core, a Gemini at its finest.

The King and Queen of my mental palace!

4/3/23

I pour blood of blue, black clouds tainting my
sky.
I talk of the stars as I always have,
but the language of mysticism is harder to
remember.
With blistering silver on the cosmos within the
depths of my heart.
Alas, no telescope in sight-
but you can't blame a girl to dream of the
universe.

Today always seems to last until the
afterthought.

4/10/23

I cannot wait until I completly breakthrough
myself.

It feels like my hand broke through this wall in
my soul.
A fist?
A helping hand?
Medicine?

Maybe it's a modality of it all.

I am not graceful with healing-
I act in full beauty and care.

I am getting better, I am getting better.

4/16/23

I am in fact just a girl, one individual woman.
Interestingly it feels as though I have three
different people's emotions.
An everlasting cycle of devil's advocacy in my
mind.

Back and forth,
Up and down,
Far and near,
and everywhere all at once

It feels like every crevice in my mind has been
tainted, but not by me.
Or at least I do not remember.
A constant loop of anything and everything.

I am trying, but maybe that is the problem. I
cannot stop trying.
But how can I let myself fully plumet?
I think I am too stubborn to not step in and save
myself.
Who else will?

The rational and reasonable side of myself
knows I am loved, cherished, worthy, and
valued.

Deep down I know that there is a version of
myself that is still deeply wounded, and she does
not accept this.

4/19/23

I feel like I always journal after midnight.
It is always when the moon is high in the sky
and so is my mind, that I want to write to my
heart down on Earth.
My heart loves to witness the pen on paper.

I wonder if poets consider themselves as poetic?
Sylvia Plath would probably think that is cliche.

I am just in my little world with my little pen
and my huge mind and even bigger heart.

I will be proud of what I create, vulnerable love
that does not seek validation from anyone other
than myself.

5/16/23

I will be 21 in exactly a month.
Time is really strange and I think I am scared.
My birthday is exactly a month away, however I
do not feel as uncomfortable as I usually am
during this time.
Knocking on mahogany.

I owe it to myself.
Past, present, and future.

Keaghan-
what a blessing it is to approach being 21.
I want you to know I am proud of you, and I
trust who I will be at 21.
I can see you smiling at this entry.
(Im praying!)

I know I will be right where I need to be as I hit
certain milestones in life-
things, plans, and people change just as fast as
time does.

5/17/23

Highs and lows come just as Mother Nature
does.
Which is a lot.

In the reality of my mind, I pray to be Mother
Nature and influence the seasons of my
conscious.

The moon is in Aries, and I have been building
momentum to get to this point in my life.
I am greater than these limiting experiences.

Do not let shame distract me from what truly
makes me happy.
I am proud of my passions.

5/18/23

I must accept forgiveness within myself to
experience progress.
I am not running out of time.

Is it admiral or sad how much peace I can find
when I am alone?

I do not need to feel this heavy, but it is okay to
not feel weightless.

5/20/23

There are so many analogies and excerpts that
connect the feeling of seeing the sky as a
reminder of someone they love?
I see love for everyone in everything.

My friends in movies.
My mother in laughter.
My loved ones in songs.

But I cannot recall someone I love more than
seeing the sunset.
Or the midnight sky.
Or even a quiet still moment in the morning
dew-
It simply reminds me of peace.

I yearn for that remembrance.

7/10/23

Dear Me,

It felt before that I felt no love only ambition,
not it feels the opposite.
I find the longer I have lost myself the more
content I feel.

So am I rediscovering or refurbishing?

I am lonely, but I am starting to grasp happiness.
I am breathing.
I am alive.

I am on the verge of the breakthrough!

To breathe without heaviness flooding my lungs,
To take steps and not wince of the sound of
creating movement.

I deserve my place in the world.

Noone is trained in love- they learn it as they
feel it.